What the
BIBLE
Says
about
GRIEVING

What the
BIBLE
Says
about
GRIEVING

BARBOUR
PUBLISHING

Scripture quotations marked NIV are taken from the HOLY BIBLE, NEW INTERNATIONAL VERSION®. NIV®. Copyright © 1973, 1978, 1984 by International Bible Society. Used by permission of Zondervan. All rights reserved.

Scripture quotations marked NLT are taken from the *Holy Bible*, New Living Translation, copyright © 1996, 2004. Used by permission of Tyndale House Publishers, Inc. Wheaton, Illinois 60189, U.S.A. All rights reserved.

Scripture quotations marked CEV are from the Contemporary English Version, Copyright © 1991, 1992, 1995 by American Bible Society. Used by permission.

Scripture quotations marked NKJV are taken from the New King James Version®. Copyright © 1982 by Thomas Nelson, Inc. Used by permission. All rights reserved.

Scripture quotations marked MSG are from *THE MESSAGE*. Copyright © by Eugene H. Peterson 1993, 1994, 1995, 1996, 2000, 2001, 2002. Used by permission of NavPress Publishing Group.

Scripture quotations marked NRSV are taken from the New Revised Standard Version Bible, copyright © 1989, Division of Christian Education of the National Council of the Churches of Christ in the United States of America. Used by permission. All rights reserved.

Scripture quotations marked ESV are taken from The Holy Bible, English Standard Version®, copyright © 2001 by Crossway Bibles, a publishing ministry of Good News Publishers. Used by permission. All rights reserved.

Published by Barbour Publishing, Inc., P.O. Box 719, Uhrichsville, Ohio 44683, www.barbourbooks.com

Our mission is to publish and distribute inspirational products offering exceptional value and biblical encouragement to the masses.

CONTENTS

INTRODUCTION

UNINVITED GRIEF

The heartache of grief can come from many places: a death, a divorce, or even the loss of a dream. These losses can cause tremendous disappointment and pain. And while these dark valleys change our lives forever, we are not meant to wallow in a state of endless depression. Instead, the process of grieving can keep us from becoming permanently crippled by loss, helping us to continue to walk through it.

Counselors have identified five stages of grief: (1) denial, (2) anger, (3) guilt, (4) depression, and (5) acceptance. Each stage represents a natural response to loss. People who are grieving will work through these stages in their own order and on their own timetable. While this book is not a road map through these stages, it does contain verses that can strengthen your spirit

9

as you experience this difficult time. Turn the pages of this book and begin to find ways God's Word can be a salve to your wounded spirit.

CHAPTER 1

YOU'RE NOT ALONE

I sat numbly at my husband's graveside and wished for the pain to go away. I wanted so badly to share the heartache with my best friend. But that friend now lay lifeless, unable to listen or respond to the pain his death had caused me. He had left this life without a final good-bye, and I just wasn't ready to part ways. I had much more to tell him, and we had much more life to share. In the days to come, it meant so much to have other people around. And while they couldn't take away the pain, it was nice to have people nearby even if they were only able to listen, hug, and cry along with me.

■ Stacey, age 42, Minnesota ■

BELIEVING IN A GOD WHO CARES

■ You don't need to cry anymore. The LORD is kind, and as soon as he hears your cries for help, he will come.

ISAIAH 30:19 CEV

■ For this is what the high and lofty One says—he who lives forever, whose name is holy:
"I live in a high and holy place, but also with him who is contrite and lowly in spirit,
to revive the spirit of the lowly and to revive the heart of the contrite."

ISAIAH 57:15 NIV

■ You notice everything I do and everywhere I go.

PSALM 139:3 CEV

GOD keeps an eye on his friends,
his ears pick up every moan and groan.

PSALM 34:15 MSG

He reached down from on high and took
hold of me; he drew me out of deep waters.

PSALM 18:16 NIV

I'm still in your presence,
but you've taken my hand.
You wisely and tenderly lead me,
and then you bless me.

PSALM 73:23–24 MSG

Come near to God and he will come near
to you.

JAMES 4:8 NIV

■ The beloved of the LORD rests in safety—
the High God surrounds him all day long—
the beloved rests between his shoulders.

DEUTERONOMY 33:12 NRSV

■ "The young women will dance for joy, and
the men—old and young—will join in the
celebration. I will turn their mourning into joy.
I will comfort them and exchange their
sorrow for rejoicing."

JEREMIAH 31:13 NLT

■ Whom have I in heaven but you? And earth
has nothing I desire besides you.

PSALM 73:25 NIV

FOLLOWING A GOD WHO KNOWS YOUR PAIN

■ "Though he slay me, yet will I hope in him."

JOB 13:15 NIV

■ Praise be to the God and Father of our Lord Jesus Christ, the Father of compassion and the God of all comfort, who comforts us in all our troubles, so that we can comfort those in any trouble with the comfort we ourselves have received from God. For just as the sufferings of Christ flow over into our lives, so also through Christ our comfort overflows.

2 CORINTHIANS 1:3–5 NIV

■ Because God's children are human beings—made of flesh and blood—the Son also became flesh and blood. For only as a human being could he die, and only by dying could he break the power of the devil, who had the power of death. Only in this way could he set free all who have lived their lives as slaves to the fear of dying.

We also know that the Son did not come to help angels; he came to help the descendants of Abraham. Therefore, it was necessary for him to be made in every respect like us, his brothers and sisters, so that he could be our merciful and faithful High Priest before God. Then he could offer a sacrifice that would take away the sins of the people. Since he himself has gone through suffering and testing, he is able to help us when we are being tested.

HEBREWS 2:14–18 NLT

Therefore he is able to save completely those who come to God through him, because he always lives to intercede for them.

HEBREWS 7:25 NIV

He was despised and rejected by men,
    a man of sorrows, and familiar with
    suffering.
Like one from whom men hide their faces
    he was despised, and we esteemed
    him not.

ISAIAH 53:3 NIV

CRYING OUT TO GOD

■ "Until now you have not asked for anything in my name. Ask and you will receive, and your joy will be complete."

JOHN 16:24 NIV

■ "Which of you, if his son asks for bread, will give him a stone? Or if he asks for a fish, will give him a snake? If you, then, though you are evil, know how to give good gifts to your children, how much more will your Father in heaven give good gifts to those who ask him!"

MATTHEW 7:9–11 NIV

■ "And if God cares so wonderfully for flowers that are here today and thrown into the fire tomorrow, he will certainly care for you. Why do you have so little faith?"

LUKE 12:28 NLT

■ And we are confident that he hears us whenever we ask for anything that pleases him. And since we know he hears us when we make our requests, we also know that he will give us what we ask for.

1 JOHN 5:14–15 NLT

■ God. . .richly gives us all we need for our enjoyment.

1 TIMOTHY 6:17 NLT

■ You want something you don't have, and you will do anything to get it. You will even kill! But you still cannot get what you want, and you won't get it by fighting and arguing. You should pray for it. Yet even when you do pray, your prayers are not answered, because you pray just for selfish reasons.

JAMES 4:2–3 CEV

■ Every good and perfect gift is from above, coming down from the Father of the heavenly lights, who does not change like shifting shadows.

JAMES 1:17 NIV

■ I know what I'm doing. I have it all planned out—plans to take care of you, not abandon you, plans to give you the future you hope for.

JEREMIAH 29:11 MSG

■ Praise be to the Lord, to God our Savior, who daily bears our burdens.

PSALM 68:19 NIV

Pile your troubles on GOD's shoulders—
        he'll carry your load, he'll help you out.
He'll never let good people
        topple into ruin.

PSALM 55:22 MSG

FINDING SAFETY WITH HIM

■ "I, your GOD, have a firm grip on you and
I'm not letting go. I'm telling you, 'Don't panic.
I'm right here to help you.'"

ISAIAH 41:13 MSG

■ Don't be afraid, for I am with you.
Don't be discouraged, for I am your God.
I will strengthen you and help you.
I will hold you up with my victorious
right hand.

ISAIAH 41:10 NLT

■ You hear, O LORD, the desire of the afflicted;
you encourage them, and you listen to
their cry.

PSALM 10:17 NIV

■ The angel of the LORD encamps around those who fear him, and delivers them.

PSALM 34:7 ESV

■ "Have I not commanded you? Be strong and courageous. Do not be terrified; do not be discouraged, for the LORD your God will be with you wherever you go."

JOSHUA 1:9 NIV

■ You have allowed me to suffer much hardship, but you will restore me to life again and lift me up from the depths of the earth.

PSALM 71:20 NLT

■ God is our refuge and strength, an ever-present help in trouble.

Therefore we will not fear, though the earth give way and the mountains fall into the heart of the sea, though its waters roar and foam and the mountains quake with their surging.

PSALM 46:1–3 NIV

ALLOWING FRIENDS TO CARE

■ Bear one another's burdens, and so fulfill the law of Christ.

GALATIANS 6:2 ESV

■ It's better to have a partner than go it alone.
Share the work, share the wealth.
And if one falls down, the other helps,
But if there's no one to help, tough!
Two in a bed warm each other.
Alone, you shiver all night.
By yourself you're unprotected.
With a friend you can face the worst.
Can you round up a third?
A three-stranded rope isn't easily snapped.

ECCLESIASTES 4:9–12 MSG

■ Jesus answered: Love the Lord your God with all your heart, soul, and mind. This is the first and most important commandment. The second most important commandment is like this one. And it is, "Love others as much as you love yourself." All the Law of Moses and the Books of the Prophets are based on these two commandments.

MATTHEW 22:37–40 CEV

■ God put our bodies together in such a way that even the parts that seem the least important are valuable. He did this to make all parts of the body work together smoothly, with each part caring about the others. If one part of our body hurts, we hurt all over. If one part of our body is honored, the whole body will be happy.

1 CORINTHIANS 12:24–26 CEV

JOINING THE UNIVERSAL EXPERIENCE

■ "People are born for trouble as readily as sparks fly up from a fire."

JOB 5:7 NLT

■ "How frail is humanity!
How short is life, how full of trouble!"

JOB 14:1 NLT

■ So what do people get in this life for all their hard work and anxiety?

ECCLESIASTES 2:22 NLT

■ We all come to the end of our lives as naked and empty-handed as on the day we were born. We can't take our riches with us.

And this, too, is a very serious problem. People leave this world no better off than when they came. All their hard work is for nothing—like working for the wind. Throughout their lives, they live under a cloud—frustrated, discouraged, and angry.

ECCLESIASTES 5:15–17 NLT

■ "Naked I came from my mother's womb,
    and naked I will depart.
The LORD gave and the LORD has taken away;
    may the name of the LORD be praised."

JOB 1:21 NIV

■ Yet you brought me out of the womb;
>   you made me trust in you even
>   at my mother's breast.
From birth I was cast upon you;
>   from my mother's womb you have
>   been my God.
Do not be far from me,
>   for trouble is near
>   and there is no one to help.

PSALM 22:9–11 NIV

ONE MOMENT
AT A TIME
DON'T FLY
SOLO

1. Grief is inevitable. We all are touched by significant losses at some point in our lives. Don't try to walk through the dark periods alone but seek out a friend who can sit and listen. Talking about your grief is vital.

2. Don't disconnect. Talking with others can help you keep perspective and find the support you need. Resist the temptation to retreat into your own private world.

3. God knows your pain. God knew that when death entered the world (Genesis 3), our lives would have seasons of difficulty.

He experienced pain Himself through the sufferings of Christ. God can empathize with you. Share your pain with Him.

CHAPTER 2

LIFE-CHANGING EVENTS

Within a year's time, my family experienced a lot of changes. My parents died early in the year. And while their health had been poor for a long time, the end was still very difficult for all of us. Soon after their deaths, my nephew was killed in an accident and my sister filed for divorce. In the course of this difficult year, I learned how painful life is and how healthy grieving can be.

■ Norm, age 39, Oregon ■

FEELING THE STING OF DEATH

■ Jesus told her, "I am the resurrection and the life. Anyone who believes in me will live, even after dying. Everyone who lives in me and believes in me will never ever die."

JOHN 11:25–26 NLT

■ Christ died and rose again for this very purpose—to be Lord both of the living and of the dead.

ROMANS 14:9 NLT

■ Precious in the sight of the LORD
is the death of his saints.

PSALM 116:15 ESV

■ [This grace] has now been revealed through the appearing of our Savior, Christ Jesus, who has destroyed death and has brought life and immortality to light through the gospel.

2 TIMOTHY 1:10 NIV

■ "Because of God's tender mercy, the morning light from heaven is about to break upon us, to give light to those who sit in darkness and in the shadow of death, and to guide us to the path of peace."

LUKE 1:78–79 NLT

■ Behold, the eye of the LORD is on those who fear him, on those who hope in his steadfast love, that he may deliver their soul from death and keep them alive in famine.

PSALM 33:18–19 ESV

■ And I heard a voice from heaven saying, "Write this down: Blessed are those who die in the Lord from now on. Yes, says the Spirit, they are blessed indeed, for they will rest from their hard work; for their good deeds follow them!"

REVELATION 14:13 NLT

■ For to me, living means living for Christ, and dying is even better.

PHILIPPIANS 1:21 NLT

■ We are confident, I say, and would prefer to be away from the body and at home with the Lord.

2 CORINTHIANS 5:8 NIV

■ Brothers, we do not want you to be ignorant about those who fall asleep, or to grieve like the rest of men, who have no hope.

1 THESSALONIANS 4:13 NIV

■ For what I received I passed on to you as of first importance: that Christ died for our sins according to the Scriptures, that he was buried, that he was raised on the third day according to the Scriptures. . . .

But if it is preached that Christ has been raised from the dead, how can some of you say that there is no resurrection of the dead? If there is no resurrection of the dead, then not even Christ has been raised. And if Christ has not been raised, our preaching is useless and so is your faith.

1 CORINTHIANS 15:3–4, 12–14 NIV

■ I declare to you, brothers, that flesh and blood cannot inherit the kingdom of God, nor does the perishable inherit the imperishable. Listen, I tell you a mystery: We will not all sleep, but we will all be changed—in a flash, in the twinkling of an eye, at the last trumpet. For the trumpet will sound, the dead will be raised imperishable, and we will be changed. For the perishable must clothe itself with the imperishable, and the mortal with immortality. When the perishable has been clothed with the imperishable, and the mortal with immortality, then the saying that is written will come true: "Death has been swallowed up in victory."

"Where, O death, is your victory?
Where, O death, is your sting?"

1 CORINTHIANS 15:50–55 NIV

Someone may ask, "How are the dead raised? With what kind of body will they come?" . . . The body that is sown is perishable, it is raised imperishable; it is sown in dishonor, it is raised in glory; it is sown in weakness, it is raised in power; it is sown a natural body, it is raised a spiritual body.

1 CORINTHIANS 15:35, 42–44 NIV

LOSING A DREAM

■ "So do not worry, saying, 'What shall we
eat?' or 'What shall we drink?' or 'What shall
we wear?' For the pagans run after all these
things, and your heavenly Father knows that
you need them. But seek first his kingdom
and his righteousness, and all these things
will be given to you as well. Therefore do
not worry about tomorrow, for tomorrow
will worry about itself. Each day has enough
trouble of its own."

MATTHEW 6:31–34 NIV

■ Yes, we should make the most of what God
gives, both the bounty and the capacity to
enjoy it, accepting what's given and delighting
in the work. It's God's gift!

ECCLESIASTES 5:19 MSG

■ God, I beg two favors from you;
let me have them before I die.
First, help me never to tell a lie.
Second, give me neither poverty nor
    riches!
Give me just enough to satisfy my needs.
For if I grow rich, I may deny you and say,
    "Who is the LORD?"
And if I am too poor, I may steal and thus
insult God's holy name.

PROVERBS 30:7–9 NLT

■ God is there, ready to help;
I'm fearless no matter what.
Who or what can get to me?

HEBREWS 13:6 MSG

41

■ For this is what the LORD says. . .
"As a mother comforts her child,
so will I comfort you. . . ."
When you see this, your heart will rejoice
and you will flourish like grass;
the hand of the LORD will be made
known to his servants,
but his fury will be shown to his foes.

ISAIAH 66:12–14 NIV

■ The LORD is my shepherd, I shall not be
in want.
He makes me lie down in green pastures,
he leads me beside quiet waters,
he restores my soul.
He guides me in paths of righteousness
for his name's sake.

PSALM 23:1–3 NIV

■ But Zion said, "I don't get it. GOD has left me.
My Master has forgotten I even exist."
"Can a mother forget the infant at her breast,
    walk away from the baby she bore?
But even if mothers forget,
    I'd never forget you—never.
Look, I've written your names on the backs
    of my hands.
The walls you're rebuilding are never out of
    my sight.
Your builders are faster than your wreckers.
    The demolition crews are gone for good.
Look up, look around, look well!
    See them all gathering, coming to you?
As sure as I am the living God"—GOD's
    Decree—"you're going to put them on
    like so much jewelry, you're going to use
    them to dress up like a bride."

ISAIAH 49:14–18 MSG

FACING ILLNESS

■ Be humble in the presence of God's mighty power, and he will honor you when the time comes. God cares for you, so turn all your worries over to him.

1 PETER 5:6–7 CEV

■ For his Spirit joins with our spirit to affirm that we are God's children. And since we are his children, we are his heirs. In fact, together with Christ we are heirs of God's glory. But if we are to share his glory, we must also share his suffering. Yet what we suffer now is nothing compared to the glory he will reveal to us later.

ROMANS 8:16–18 NLT

■ The LORD hears his people when they call
  to him for help.
He rescues them from all their troubles.
The LORD is close to the brokenhearted;
  he rescues those whose spirits are
  crushed.

PSALM 34:17–18 NLT

■ We wait in hope for the LORD;
  he is our help and our shield.
In him our hearts rejoice,
  for we trust in his holy name.
May your unfailing love rest upon us, O LORD,
  even as we put our hope in you.

PSALM 33:20–22 NIV

■ As he went along, he saw a man blind from birth. His disciples asked him, "Rabbi, who sinned, this man or his parents, that he was born blind?"

"Neither this man nor his parents sinned," said Jesus, "but this happened so that the work of God might be displayed in his life."

JOHN 9:1–3 NIV

■ Each time he said, "My grace is all you need. My power works best in weakness." So now I am glad to boast about my weaknesses, so that the power of Christ can work through me. That's why I take pleasure in my weaknesses, and in the insults, hardships, persecutions, and troubles that I suffer for Christ. For when I am weak, then I am strong.

2 CORINTHIANS 12:9–10 NLT

■ "LORD, remind me how brief my time on
        earth will be.
Remind me that my days are
        numbered—how fleeting my life is.
You have made my life no longer than
        the width of my hand.
My entire lifetime is just a moment
        to you; at best, each of us is but a breath."
We are merely moving shadows,
        and all our busy rushing ends in nothing.
We heap up wealth,
        not knowing who will spend it.
And so, Lord, where do I put my hope?
        My only hope is in you.

PSALM 39:4 – 7 NLT

You, LORD, are the one I praise.
So heal me and rescue me!
Then I will be completely well and
    perfectly safe.

JEREMIAH 17:14 CEV

DEALING WITH DIVORCE

■ My flesh and my heart fail;
>   but God is the strength of my heart
>   and my portion forever.

PSALM 73:26 NKJV

■ If we are faithless,
>   he will remain faithful,
>   for he cannot disown himself.

2 TIMOTHY 2:13 NIV

■ He has never let you down,
>   never looked the other way
>   when you were being kicked around.
>   He has never wandered off to do his
>   own thing; he has been right there,
>   listening.

PSALM 22:24 MSG

■ Now to him who is able to keep you from stumbling and to present you blameless before the presence of his glory with great joy, to the only God, our Savior, through Jesus Christ our Lord, be glory, majesty, dominion, and authority, before all time and now and forever. Amen.

JUDE 1:24–25 ESV

■ "The LORD will fight for you; you need only to be still."

EXODUS 14:14 NIV

■ That is why I am suffering as I am. Yet I am not ashamed, because I know whom I have believed, and am convinced that he is able to guard what I have entrusted to him for that day.

2 TIMOTHY 1:12 NIV

■ As the Scripture says, "Anyone who trusts in him will never be put to shame."

ROMANS 10:11 NIV

■ "Do not be afraid; you will not suffer shame.
Do not fear disgrace; you will not be
    humiliated.
You will forget the shame of your youth
    and remember no more the reproach
    of your widowhood."

ISAIAH 54:4 NIV

■ So now there is no condemnation for those who belong to Christ Jesus.

ROMANS 8:1 NLT

■ Let us fix our eyes on Jesus, the author and perfecter of our faith, who for the joy set before him endured the cross, scorning its shame, and sat down at the right hand of the throne of God. Consider him who endured such opposition from sinful men, so that you will not grow weary and lose heart.

HEBREWS 12:2–3 NIV

EXPERIENCING THE LOSS OF A CHILD

■ Then little children were brought to Jesus for him to place his hands on them and pray for them. But the disciples rebuked those who brought them.

Jesus said, "Let the little children come to me, and do not hinder them, for the kingdom of heaven belongs to such as these."

MATTHEW 19:13–14 NIV

■ Jesus called them back. "Let these children alone. Don't get between them and me. These children are the kingdom's pride and joy."

LUKE 18:16 MSG

For you created my inmost being;
you knit me together in my mother's
womb.

I praise you because I am fearfully
and wonderfully made; your works are
wonderful, I know that full well. . . .

Your eyes saw my unformed body.

All the days ordained for me were
written in your book before one of them
came to be.

PSALM 139:13–14, 16 NIV

"But now, Lord, what do I look for?
My hope is in you."

PSALM 39:7 NIV

Let your steadfast love comfort me
according to your promise to your servant.

PSALM 119:76 ESV

SAYING GOOD-BYE TO A PARENT

■ Even if my father and mother abandon me, the Lord will hold me close.

PSALM 27:10 NLT

■ God sets the lonely in families, he leads forth the prisoners with singing; but the rebellious live in a sun-scorched land.

PSALM 68:6 NIV

■ "I will be a Father to you, and you will be my sons and daughters, says the Lord Almighty."

2 CORINTHIANS 6:18 NIV

■ "No, I will not abandon you as orphans—
I will come to you."

JOHN 14:18 NLT

■ God assured us, "I'll never let you down,
never walk off and leave you."

HEBREWS 13:5 MSG

ONE MOMENT
AT A TIME
MEETING A LIFE CHANGE

1. Grieve the loss. Losing a job or having a marriage fall apart can seem minor compared to the death of a family member. And while your situation may not seem as severe as someone else's, grieving is still productive. It is important to work through each emotion and understand what you are feeling so that you can find the closure you need.

2. Don't venture alone. If you are facing an illness, divorce, or the loss of a family member, help may be available. Consider attending a grief support group, and talk to others who

are going through—or have gone through—
similar situations.

3. Consider becoming a volunteer. Nursing
homes and children's hospitals are filled
with hurting people. Your experience and
ability to empathize may be what other
families need.

CHAPTER 3

ASSAULTED BY ANGER

Before my daughter's death, I wasn't an angry person. But losing her changed everything, and overnight I was filled with anger as I have never experienced it before. I'm angry at her for sneaking out the night she died. I'm angry at the drunk driver who caused the accident. I'm angry at God who let all this happen during His watch. It isn't fair! I can't understand why all this would happen. Why, God? Why?

■ Yolanda, age 44, West Virginia ■

DEALING WITH ANGER

■ Be patient and trust the LORD.
Don't let it bother you when all goes well
for those who do sinful things.
Don't be angry or furious. Anger can lead
to sin.

PSALM 37:7–8 CEV

■ Don't befriend angry people
or associate with hot-tempered people,
or you will learn to be like them
and endanger your soul.

PROVERBS 22:24–25 NLT

■ Beloved, never avenge yourselves, but leave it to the wrath of God, for it is written, "Vengeance is mine, I will repay, says the Lord." To the contrary, "if your enemy is hungry, feed him; if he is thirsty, give him something to drink; for by so doing you will heap burning coals on his head." Do not be overcome by evil, but overcome evil with good.

ROMANS 12:19–21 ESV

■ Let all bitterness and wrath and anger and clamor and slander be put away from you, along with all malice.

EPHESIANS 4:31 ESV

■ Better to be patient than powerful;
better to have self-control than to
conquer a city.

PROVERBS 16:32 NLT

■ Fools have short fuses and explode all too
quickly; the prudent quietly shrug off insults.

PROVERBS 12:16 MSG

■ My dear brothers, take note of this: Everyone
should be quick to listen, slow to speak and
slow to become angry.

JAMES 1:19 NIV

EXTENDING FORGIVENESS TO OTHERS

■ Dear friends, let us continue to love one another, for love comes from God. Anyone who loves is a child of God and knows God. But anyone who does not love does not know God, for God is love.

1 JOHN 4:7–8 NLT

■ Be gentle with one another, sensitive. Forgive one another as quickly and thoroughly as God in Christ forgave you.

EPHESIANS 4:32 MSG

■ Then Peter came to Jesus and asked, "Lord, how many times shall I forgive my brother when he sins against me? Up to seven times?"

Jesus answered, "I tell you, not seven times, but seventy-seven times."

MATTHEW 18:21–22 NIV

■ "And when you stand praying, if you hold anything against anyone, forgive him, so that your Father in heaven may forgive you your sins."

MARK 11:25 NIV

COMBATING BITTERNESS

Don't grumble against each other, brothers,
or you will be judged. The Judge is standing
at the door!

JAMES 5:9 NIV

Above all else, guard your heart,
for it is the wellspring of life.

PROVERBS 4:23 NIV

See to it that no one misses the grace of
God and that no bitter root grows up to
cause trouble and defile many.

HEBREWS 12:15 NIV

■ Anyone who claims to be in the light but hates his brother is still in the darkness. Whoever loves his brother lives in the light, and there is nothing in him to make him stumble. But whoever hates his brother is in the darkness and walks around in the darkness; he does not know where he is going, because the darkness has blinded him.

1 JOHN 2:9–11 NIV

People may cover their hatred with pleasant
    words, but they're deceiving you.
They pretend to be kind, but don't
    believe them.
Their hearts are full of many evils.
While their hatred may be concealed
    by trickery, their wrongdoing will
    be exposed in public.

PROVERBS 26:24–26 NLT

ONE MOMENT
AT A TIME

UNDERSTANDING
ANGER

1. Don't apologize for how you feel.
Anger during a time of grieving is normal.
Give yourself permission, if needed, to
feel angry.

2. Let it out. Keeping anger pent up inside
you can turn you into a time bomb just
waiting to explode at the most inappropriate
moments. Find productive ways to release
your emotions.

3. Be honest with God. While it can be un-
nerving to find yourself angry with God, you
can be honest with Him about how you feel.

Reading the Psalms will help you find many places David vented to God honestly yet reverently. See Psalm 22, for example.

4. Consider joining a support group. Meeting with others who can empathize can help you. And being able to help others will aid you, too.

CHAPTER 4

WRESTLING WITH GUILT

I should have tried to make things right.
I should have let him know how I really felt.
I should have been a better friend.
I shouldn't have held back so much.
I spent entire days beating myself up with
thoughts like these. I finally had to come
to terms with myself: I'm human, and yes,
I've failed. . .but God forgives.

■ Wayne, age 69, Illinois ■

EMBRACING FORGIVENESS

■ If we confess our sins, he is faithful and just
and will forgive us our sins and purify us from
all unrighteousness.

1 JOHN 1:9 NIV

■ In him we have redemption through his
blood, the forgiveness of sins, in accordance
with the riches of God's grace that he
lavished on us with all wisdom and
understanding.

EPHESIANS 1:7–8 NIV

Therefore, if anyone is in Christ, he is a new creation; the old has gone, the new has come! All this is from God, who reconciled us to himself through Christ and gave us the ministry of reconciliation: that God was reconciling the world to himself in Christ, not counting men's sins against them. And he has committed to us the message of reconciliation. We are therefore Christ's ambassadors, as though God were making his appeal through us. We implore you on Christ's behalf: Be reconciled to God. God made him who had no sin to be sin for us, so that in him we might become the righteousness of God.

2 CORINTHIANS 5:17–21 NIV

■ He personally carried our sins
    in his body on the cross
so that we can be dead to sin
    and live for what is right.
By his wounds
    you are healed.

1 PETER 2:24 NLT

■ God rescued us from dead-end alleys
and dark dungeons. He's set us up in the
kingdom of the Son he loves so much, the
Son who got us out of the pit we were in,
got rid of the sins we were doomed to
keep repeating.

COLOSSIANS 1:13–14 MSG

My little children, I am writing these things to you so that you may not sin. But if anyone does sin, we have an advocate with the Father, Jesus Christ the righteous.

1 JOHN 2:1 NRSV

Help us, O God of our salvation!
  Help us for the glory of your name.
Save us and forgive our sins
  for the honor of your name.

PSALM 79:9 NLT

But you, O Lord, are a compassionate and gracious God, slow to anger, abounding in love and faithfulness.

PSALM 86:15 NIV

Praise the LORD, O my soul;

>   all my inmost being, praise his holy name.

Praise the LORD, O my soul,

>   and forget not all his benefits—

who forgives all your sins

>   and heals all your diseases,

who redeems your life from the pit

>   and crowns you with love and compassion.

PSALM 103:1–4 NIV

LETTING GO OF YOUR GUILT

■ As far as the east is from the west,
so far does he remove our transgressions
from us.

PSALM 103:12 ESV

■ "Come now, let's settle this,"
says the LORD.
"Though your sins are like scarlet,
I will make them as white as snow.
Though they are red like crimson,
I will make them as white as wool."

ISAIAH 1:18 NLT

■ "I—yes, I alone—will blot out your sins for my own sake and will never think of them again."

ISAIAH 43:25 NLT

■ Don't stay far away, LORD!
My strength comes from you, so hurry
    and help.
Rescue me from enemy swords
    and save me from those dogs.
Don't let lions eat me.
You rescued me from the horns of wild bulls.

PSALM 22:19–21 CEV

■ Not that I have already obtained all this, or have already been made perfect, but I press on to take hold of that for which Christ Jesus took hold of me.

PHILIPPIANS 3:12 NIV

"Be still, and know that I am God;
I will be exalted among the nations,
I will be exalted in the earth."

PSALM 46:10 NIV

ONE MOMENT
AT A TIME
GUILT BUSTERS

1. Free yourself from false guilt. False guilt can hinder your recovery if you unreasonably blame yourself for things you did or didn't do.

2. Say you're sorry. Because you are human, you may have legitimate guilt about things you have said, done, or not done. And while you can no longer address that person directly, it can be healthy to release what you are feeling. Write your loved one a letter. Visit the graveside to say you're sorry. And while you may wish to go backward in time and do something differently, that choice isn't an option. In the end, the only thing you may be able to do is choose to let go of the guilt or resentment.

3. Allow yourself to live. Many people feel guilty for laughing or finding enjoyment during their time of grief. It's okay to take a break from the pain. Eventually you will want to find a way to resume enjoying life while treasuring the memories you hold dear.

CHAPTER 5

DEPRESSION

Grief is debilitating. After the funeral was over and everyone went home, I found myself exhausted. I didn't answer the phone, and on most days, I didn't even go outside to get the mail. And while my boss expected me back at work a few days later, I couldn't bring myself to go back so quickly. I ended up losing the job but found that I didn't care anymore. I'm doing better now, though. And through all this, I have been able to survive because I remember that God cares and that this pain will eventually pass.

■ Reginald, age 26, North Carolina ■

FEELING DEPRESSION

I waited patiently for the L<small>ORD</small> to help me,
   and he turned to me and heard my cry.
He lifted me out of the pit of despair,
   out of the mud and the mire.
He set my feet on solid ground
   and steadied me as I walked along.

P<small>SALM</small> 40:1 – 2 <small>NLT</small>

Yet you are enthroned as the Holy One;
   you are the praise of Israel.
In you our fathers put their trust;
   they trusted and you delivered them.
They cried to you and were saved;
   in you they trusted and were not
   disappointed.

P<small>SALM</small> 22:3 – 5 <small>NIV</small>

■ See how very much our Father loves us, for he calls us his children, and that is what we are!

1 JOHN 3:1 NLT

■ "The LORD your God is with you,
 he is mighty to save.
He will take great delight in you,
 he will quiet you with his love,
 he will rejoice over you with singing."

ZEPHANIAH 3:17 NIV

■ "He cuts off every branch in me that bears no fruit, while every branch that does bear fruit he prunes so that it will be even more fruitful."

JOHN 15:2 NIV

■ "I have told you these things, so that in me you may have peace. In this world you will have trouble. But take heart! I have overcome the world."

JOHN 16:33 NIV

■ "Ask and it will be given to you; seek and you will find; knock and the door will be opened to you. For everyone who asks receives; he who seeks finds; and to him who knocks, the door will be opened."

MATTHEW 7:7–8 NIV

For his anger lasts only a moment,
    but his favor lasts a lifetime;
weeping may remain for a night,
    but rejoicing comes in the morning.

PSALM 30:5 NIV

BEING ALONE

"And lo, I am with you always, even to the end of the age."

MATTHEW 28:20 NKJV

"It is the LORD who goes before you. He will be with you; he will not leave you or forsake you. Do not fear or be dismayed."

DEUTERONOMY 31:8 ESV

Turn to me and be gracious to me,
    for I am lonely and afflicted.
The troubles of my heart have multiplied;
    free me from my anguish.

PSALM 25:16–17 NIV

■ "For the sake of his great name the LORD will not reject his people, because the LORD was pleased to make you his own."

1 SAMUEL 12:22 NIV

■ Even though I walk through the valley
    of the shadow of death,
I will fear no evil,
    for you are with me;
your rod and your staff,
    they comfort me.

PSALM 23:4 NIV

■ I will be glad and rejoice in your love,
    for you saw my affliction
    and knew the anguish of my soul.

PSALM 31:7 NIV

■ But I trust in you, O LORD;
  I say, "You are my God."
My times are in your hands;
  deliver me from my enemies
  and from those who pursue me.

PSALM 31:14–15 NIV

■ For the LORD your God is a merciful God; he
will not abandon or destroy you or forget
the covenant with your forefathers, which he
confirmed to them by oath.

DEUTERONOMY 4:31 NIV

■ "I am not alone, for my Father is with me."

JOHN 16:32 NIV

CRYING WITH A BROKEN HEART

■ We are hard pressed on every side, but not crushed; perplexed, but not in despair; persecuted, but not abandoned; struck down, but not destroyed. We always carry around in our body the death of Jesus, so that the life of Jesus may also be revealed in our body.

2 CORINTHIANS 4:8–10 NIV

■ Trust in him at all times, O people;
pour out your hearts to him,
for God is our refuge.

PSALM 62:8 NIV

■   "Don't be afraid, I've redeemed you.
I've called your name. You're mine.
When you're in over your head, I'll be
    there with you.
When you're in rough waters, you will
    not go down.
When you're between a rock and a hard
    place, it won't be a dead end—
    because I am GOD, your personal God,
    the Holy of Israel, your Savior.
I paid a huge price for you: all of Egypt,
    with rich Cush and Seba thrown in!
That's how much you mean to me!
That's how much I love you!
I'd sell off the whole world to get you back,
    trade the creation just for you."

ISAIAH 43:1–4 MSG

What, then, shall we say in response to this? If God is for us, who can be against us? He who did not spare his own Son, but gave him up for us all—how will he not also, along with him, graciously give us all things? Who will bring any charge against those whom God has chosen? It is God who justifies. Who is he that condemns? Christ Jesus, who died— more than that, who was raised to life—is at the right hand of God and is also interceding for us. Who shall separate us from the love of Christ? Shall trouble or hardship or persecution or famine or nakedness or danger or sword? As it is written:

"For your sake we face death all day long; we are considered as sheep to be slaughtered."

No, in all these things we are more than conquerors through him who loved us.

ROMANS 8:31–37 NIV

 The LORD God is waiting to show how kind
he is and to have pity on you.
The LORD always does right;
he blesses those who trust him.

ISAIAH 30:18 CEV

LIVING WITH ANXIETY

■ God cares for you, so turn all your worries over to him.

1 PETER 5:7 CEV

■ Trust in the LORD with all your heart
    and lean not on your own understanding;
in all your ways acknowledge him,
    and he will make your paths straight.

PROVERBS 3:5–6 NIV

■ "Your Father knows exactly what you need even before you ask him!"

MATTHEW 6:8 NLT

■ "What is the price of five sparrows—two copper coins? Yet God does not forget a single one of them. And the very hairs on your head are all numbered. So don't be afraid; you are more valuable to God than a whole flock of sparrows."

LUKE 12:6–7 NLT

■ "Can all your worries add a single moment to your life? And if worry can't accomplish a little thing like that, what's the use of worrying over bigger things?"

LUKE 12:25–26 NLT

■ Trust in the LORD and do good;
    dwell in the land and enjoy safe pasture.
Delight yourself in the LORD
    and he will give you the desires of your heart.

PSALM 37:3–4 NIV

Even strong young lions sometimes go hungry, but those who trust in the LORD will lack no good thing.

PSALM 34:10 NLT

ONE MOMENT
AT A TIME

KEEPING
THE MEMORY
ALIVE

1. Keep moving. Don't allow yourself to spiral endlessly downward. Create a short list of things to do and make sure you complete at least one productive task each day.

2. Add walking to your schedule. The chemical changes that happen in your body as you exercise can be a healthy way to clear your mind and reinvigorate your heart.

3. Journal. Write about episodes that make you laugh or cry, or simply capture the character and personality of the person you remember.

CHAPTER 6

THE RECOVERY PROCESS

I think that someone who hasn't really encountered grief can't understand what people call "recovery." The truth is I will never fully recover. I work hard, and every day is easier than the last one, but I'll never be the person I was before this happened. Honestly, I don't know if I'd want to be. While the pain has been difficult, I'm a better person for having gone through this experience.

■ Ryan, age 61, Oklahoma ■

FINDING HEALING

■ Beloved, do not be surprised at the fiery
ordeal that is taking place among you to
test you, as though something strange were
happening to you. But rejoice insofar as you
are sharing Christ's sufferings, so that you may
also be glad and shout for joy when his glory
is revealed.

1 PETER 4:12–13 NRSV

■ O LORD my God, I cried to you for help,
and you have healed me.

PSALM 30:2 NRSV

■ Heal me, O LORD, and I shall be healed;
save me, and I shall be saved,
for You are my praise.

JEREMIAH 17:14 NKJV

■ "Blessed are you who are poor, for yours is the kingdom of God.

　"Blessed are you who are hungry now, for you shall be satisfied.

　"Blessed are you who weep now, for you shall laugh."

LUKE 6:20–21 ESV

■ Therefore we do not lose heart. Though outwardly we are wasting away, yet inwardly we are being renewed day by day.

2 CORINTHIANS 4:16 NIV

■ "I will heal my people and will let them enjoy abundant peace and security."

JEREMIAH 33:6 NIV

■ We can say with confidence, "The LORD is
    my helper, so I will have no fear.
What can mere people do to me?"

HEBREWS 13:6 NLT

■ Though you have made me see troubles,
many and bitter, you will restore my life again;
from the depths of the earth you will again
bring me up.

PSALM 71:20 NIV

■ These hard times are small potatoes
compared to the coming good times,
the lavish celebration prepared for us.

2 CORINTHIANS 4:17 MSG

BECOMING A SURVIVOR

On that day you will be glad, even if you have to go through many hard trials for a while. Your faith will be like gold that has been tested in a fire. And these trials will prove that your faith is worth much more than gold that can be destroyed. They will show that you will be given praise and honor and glory when Jesus Christ returns.

You have never seen Jesus, and you don't see him now. But still you love him and have faith in him, and no words can tell how glad and happy you are to be saved. That's why you have faith.

1 PETER 1:6–9 CEV

■ Be strong and take heart,
all you who hope in the LORD.

PSALM 31:24 NIV

■ May our Lord Jesus Christ himself and God
our Father, who loved us and by his grace
gave us eternal encouragement and good
hope, encourage your hearts and strengthen
you in every good deed and word.

2 THESSALONIANS 2:16–17 NIV

■ And if the Spirit of him who raised Jesus
from the dead is living in you, he who raised
Christ from the dead will also give life to your
mortal bodies through his Spirit, who lives
in you.

ROMANS 8:11 NIV

"The thief comes only to steal and kill and destroy; I have come that they may have life, and have it to the full."

JOHN 10:10 NIV

Guide me by your truth and instruct me. You keep me safe, and I always trust you.

PSALM 25:5 CEV

MENDING YOUR SOUL

■ Nevertheless, God's solid foundation stands firm, sealed with this inscription: "The Lord knows those who are his."

2 TIMOTHY 2:19 NIV

■ Jesus answered by quoting Deuteronomy: "It takes more than bread to stay alive. It takes a steady stream of words from God's mouth."

MATTHEW 4:4 MSG

■ Oh yes, he's our God, and we're the people he pastures, the flock he feeds. Drop everything and listen, listen as he speaks.

PSALM 95:7 MSG

It is no longer I who live, but Christ lives in me. So I live in this earthly body by trusting in the Son of God, who loved me and gave himself for me.

GALATIANS 2:20 NLT

And this is the secret: Christ lives in you. This gives you assurance of sharing his glory.

COLOSSIANS 1:27 NLT

You will come to know God even better. His glorious power will make you patient and strong enough to endure anything, and you will be truly happy.

COLOSSIANS 1:10–11 CEV

■ " 'For in him we live and move and have our being.' "

ACTS 17:28 NIV

■ He heals the brokenhearted and binds up their wounds.

PSALM 147:3 NIV

COMING TO TERMS
WITH GRIEF

■ Be still in the presence of the LORD,
     and wait patiently for him to act.
Don't worry about evil people who prosper
     or fret about their wicked schemes. . . .
It is better to be godly and have little
     than to be evil and rich.

PSALM 37:7, 16 NLT

■ You keep him in perfect peace
     whose mind is stayed on you,
     because he trusts in you.
Trust in the LORD forever,
     for the LORD GOD is an everlasting rock.

ISAIAH 26:3–4 ESV

■ Rejoice in the Lord always. I will say it again: Rejoice! Let your gentleness be evident to all. The Lord is near. Do not be anxious about anything, but in everything, by prayer and petition, with thanksgiving, present your requests to God. And the peace of God, which transcends all understanding, will guard your hearts and your minds in Christ Jesus.

PHILIPPIANS 4:4–7 NIV

■ So if Christ keeps giving me his power,
I will gladly brag about how weak I am.
Yes, I am glad to be weak or insulted or
mistreated or to have troubles and sufferings,
if it is for Christ. Because when I am weak,
I am strong.

2 CORINTHIANS 12:9–10 CEV

■ I'm glad in God, far happier than you would ever guess—happy that you're again showing such strong concern for me. Not that you ever quit praying and thinking about me. You just had no chance to show it. Actually, I don't have a sense of needing anything personally. I've learned by now to be quite content whatever my circumstances. I'm just as happy with little as with much, with much as with little. I've found the recipe for being happy whether full or hungry, hands full or hands empty. Whatever I have, wherever I am, I can make it through anything in the One who makes me who I am. . . .

You can be sure that God will take care of everything you need, his generosity exceeding even yours in the glory that pours from Jesus. Our God and Father abounds in glory that just pours out into eternity. Yes.

PHILIPPIANS 4:10–13, 19–20 MSG

DISCOVERING RELIEF

■ Though an army besiege me,
  my heart will not fear;
though war break out against me,
  even then will I be confident.

PSALM 27:3 NIV

■ When I felt my feet slipping, you came with
  your love and kept me steady.
And when I was burdened with worries,
  you comforted me and made me feel
  secure.

PSALM 94:18–19 CEV

■ The LORD replied, "My Presence will go with
you, and I will give you rest."

EXODUS 33:14 NIV

■ Showing respect to the LORD brings true life—if you do it, you can relax without fear of danger.

PROVERBS 19:23 CEV

■ I sought the LORD, and he answered me; he delivered me from all my fears.

PSALM 34:4 NIV

■ Think about the things of heaven, not the things of earth. For you died to this life, and your real life is hidden with Christ in God. And when Christ, who is your life, is revealed to the whole world, you will share in all his glory.

COLOSSIANS 3:2–4 NLT

ONE MOMENT
AT A TIME

GETTING
GOING AGAIN

1. Tell their story. Share the story of your loved ones with friends and family. Sharing pictures and favorite memories is a healthy way to celebrate their memory and your connection with them.

2. Create a memory book. Assemble pictures, memories, poems, news clippings, and even a copy of your loved one's funeral service.

3. Do something your loved one would enjoy. Did your loved one have a favorite food or enjoy a favorite vacation destination?

Bring a friend and enjoy an event that your loved one would have enjoyed, as a way to honor his or her memory.

CHAPTER 7

HELPING YOUR CHILDREN GRIEVE

Having to tell my kids about their friend's death was one of the most gut-wrenching experiences of my life. Not only did they suffer through the sharp sting of loss, but their innocence was ripped away as they passed along the word of their friend's death. They have no framework yet for understanding death and its consequences. They have played so many video games I think they expect their friend to come back as easily as characters do when the letters flash "Game Over" on the screen. I wonder how many weeks it will be before they fully understand their friend is never coming back.

■ Anna, age 36, Maine ■

REDUCING THEIR LOAD

■ But Jesus said, "Let the little children come to me and do not hinder them, for to such belongs the kingdom of heaven."

MATTHEW 19:14 ESV

■ [God] comforts us in all our troubles, so that we can comfort those in any trouble with the comfort we ourselves have received from God.

2 CORINTHIANS 1:4 NIV

■ God is our refuge and strength,
   always ready to help in times of trouble.

PSALM 46:1 NLT

■ Have mercy on me, O God, have mercy
on me, for in you my soul takes refuge.

I will take refuge in the shadow of your
wings until the disaster has passed.

PSALM 57:1 NIV

■ I am surrounded by trouble, but you protect
me against my angry enemies.

With your own powerful arm you keep
me safe.

PSALM 138:7 CEV

HELPING THEM HEAL

■ Stoop down and reach out to those who are oppressed. Share their burdens, and so complete Christ's law.

GALATIANS 6:2 MSG

■ Be brave and strong! Don't be afraid. . . . The LORD your God will always be at your side, and he will never abandon you.

DEUTERONOMY 31:6 CEV

■ "Do not be terrified; do not be discouraged, for the LORD your God will be with you wherever you go."

JOSHUA 1:9 NIV

"Peace I leave with you; my peace I give to you. Not as the world gives do I give to you. Let not your hearts be troubled, neither let them be afraid."

JOHN 14:27 ESV

If your heart is broken, you'll find GOD right there; if you're kicked in the gut, he'll help you catch your breath.

PSALM 34:18 MSG

Our LORD, we belong to you.
We tell you what worries us,
    and you won't let us fall.

PSALM 55:22 CEV

■ The people of Zion said, "The LORD has turned away and forgotten us."

The LORD answered, "Could a mother forget a child who nurses at her breast?

Could she fail to love an infant who came from her own body?

Even if a mother could forget, I will never forget you.

A picture of your city is drawn on my hand.

You are always in my thoughts!"

ISAIAH 49:14–16 CEV

■ "You're blessed when you feel you've lost what is most dear to you. Only then can you be embraced by the One most dear to you."

MATTHEW 5:4 MSG

■ "Do not let your hearts be troubled. Trust in God; trust also in me. In my Father's house are many rooms; if it were not so, I would have told you. I am going there to prepare a place for you. And if I go and prepare a place for you, I will come back and take you to be with me that you also may be where I am. You know the way to the place where I am going."

JOHN 14:1 – 4 NIV

ONE MOMENT
AT A TIME

HELPING
CHILDREN
COPE

1. Teach your kids that death is part of life.
Our own fear of death as well as our desire
to protect children keeps us from teaching
kids that death is natural. It is important that
they learn about death as well as how to
grieve in a healthy way. These moments can
also become appropriate moments to share
the gospel with your children.

2. Let them see you grieve. Kids learn a lot
from parents and other adults. If they see you
remain stoic, they may learn to grieve that

way, too. But if they see you go through a full range of emotions, they may become more comfortable with their own feelings.

3. Answer their questions. Death raises a lot of questions for children. Answer them honestly and to the best of your ability. If you don't know an answer, it is okay to tell them that, too.

4. Let them talk. Talking about their loss is crucial. Let them tell stories or share things they find significant. Because children may not have the same breadth of stories, they may tell the same ones over and over again. If that's the case, let them talk freely without cutting them off.

CHAPTER 8

MINISTERING
TO OTHERS

When my husband died of cancer, I wanted to die, too. I never thought I'd make it through the dark days that followed. I'm grateful for the people who stuck with me and helped me through my pain. They helped me find joy again and encouraged me to find things to be grateful for. Once I did, I found that God began using me to provide comfort and encouragement to others who needed it. I know what it's like to be broken, and I have learned that while you can't take away another person's pain, you can listen, love, hug, pray, and encourage them with the hope that God does heal and will make them whole again.

■ Frances, age 63, Colorado ■

FINDING YOUR JOY AGAIN

■ Though the fig tree does not bud
　　and there are no grapes on the vines,
though the olive crop fails
　　and the fields produce no food,
though there are no sheep in the pen
　　and no cattle in the stalls,
yet I will rejoice in the LORD,
　　I will be joyful in God my Savior.
The Sovereign LORD is my strength;
　　he makes my feet like the feet of a deer,
　　he enables me to go on the heights.

HABAKKUK 3:17–19 NIV

■ "Now is your time of grief, but I will see you
again and you will rejoice, and no one will
take away your joy."

JOHN 16:22 NIV

Those who sow in tears
will reap with songs of joy.
He who goes out weeping,
carrying seed to sow,
will return with songs of joy,
carrying sheaves with him.

PSALM 126:5–6 NIV

Now those you have rescued will return
to Jerusalem, singing on their way.
They will be crowned with great
happiness, never again to be burdened
with sadness and sorrow.

ISAIAH 51:11 CEV

■ You have put gladness in my heart,
more than in the season that their grain
and wine increased.

PSALM 4:7 NKJV

■ Be joyful in hope, patient in affliction, faithful
in prayer.

ROMANS 12:12 NIV

■ Then my soul will rejoice in the LORD,
exulting in his salvation.

PSALM 35:9 ESV

■ But I trust in your unfailing love; my heart
rejoices in your salvation.

PSALM 13:5 NIV

134

"These things I have spoken to you,
that my joy may be in you, and that your
joy may be full."

JOHN 15:11 ESV

BEING GRATEFUL FOR LIFE

Always be joyful. Never stop praying.
Be thankful in all circumstances, for this
is God's will for you who belong to
Christ Jesus.

1 THESSALONIANS 5:16–18 NLT

Thanks be to God for his indescribable gift!

2 CORINTHIANS 9:15 NIV

"Sacrifice thank offerings to God,
fulfill your vows to the Most High."

PSALM 50:14 NIV

Shout with joy to the LORD, all the earth!
Worship the LORD with gladness.
Come before him, singing with joy.
Acknowledge that the LORD is God!
He made us, and we are his.
We are his people, the sheep of his pasture.
Enter his gates with thanksgiving;
    go into his courts with praise.
Give thanks to him and praise his name.

PSALM 100:1–4 NLT

HELPING OTHERS

■ Praise be to the God and Father of our Lord
Jesus Christ, the Father of compassion and
the God of all comfort, who comforts us
in all our troubles, so that we can comfort
those in any trouble with the comfort we
ourselves have received from God. For just
as the sufferings of Christ flow over into our
lives, so also through Christ our comfort
overflows.

2 CORINTHIANS 1:3–5 NIV

■ If one part of our body hurts, we hurt all
over. If one part of our body is honored,
the whole body will be happy.

1 CORINTHIANS 12:26 CEV

Be devoted to one another in brotherly love. Honor one another above yourselves.

ROMANS 12:10 NIV

Let's see how inventive we can be in encouraging love and helping out.

HEBREWS 10:24 MSG

Rejoice with those who rejoice; mourn with those who mourn.

ROMANS 12:15 NIV

Religion that God our Father accepts as pure and faultless is this: to look after orphans and widows in their distress and to keep oneself from being polluted by the world.

JAMES 1:27 NIV

■ "When you are harvesting your crops and forget to bring in a bundle of grain from your field, don't go back to get it. Leave it for the foreigners, orphans, and widows. Then the LORD your God will bless you in all you do. When you beat the olives from your olive trees, don't go over the boughs twice. Leave the remaining olives for the foreigners, orphans, and widows. When you gather the grapes in your vineyard, don't glean the vines after they are picked. Leave the remaining grapes for the foreigners, orphans, and widows."

DEUTERONOMY 24:19–21 NLT

■ Be rich in helping others. . .be extravagantly generous.

1 TIMOTHY 6:18 MSG

Cheerfully share your home with those who need a meal or a place to stay.

1 PETER 4:9 NLT

Each of you has been blessed with one of God's many wonderful gifts to be used in the service of others. So use your gift well.

1 PETER 4:10 CEV

ONE MOMENT
AT A TIME

JUST BE
THERE

1. Don't try to fill the silence. Sometimes it is enough to sit with the person who is grieving. Don't feel the need to come up with something profound to say. Rather, a loving smile and a tender touch are all that are needed.

2. Learn to empathize. Sympathy can come across in a condescending manner. Instead, make an effort to show empathy—which means putting yourself in the other person's shoes. Do more than simply tell someone you're sorry. Work hard at trying to enter into his or her world.

3. Pray. In the end, only God can salve a hurting heart. Sometimes the best way you can be a friend is to pray for the hurting person.

CHAPTER 9

SPIRITUAL JOURNEY

Even though I have been a pastor for a number of years, I don't always have ready answers for grieving families. Recently, as I stood at the graveside of a dear friend, I was struck with the fact that we can't answer most of our questions because we don't know enough. Really, I don't think we know enough to even ask the right questions. Death is a mystery to us. Only God sees the full picture. He alone knows what happens on the other side of eternal life and just how these events play a role in His perfect plan.

■ Jack, age 53, New York ■

QUESTIONING GOD

For my thoughts are not your thoughts,
nor are your ways my ways, says the LORD.

ISAIAH 55:8 NRSV

The suffering won't last forever. It won't be
long before this generous God who has great
plans for us in Christ—eternal and glorious
plans they are!—will have you put together
and on your feet for good.

1 PETER 5:10 MSG

"You intended to harm me, but God
intended it for good to accomplish what is
now being done, the saving of many lives."

GENESIS 50:20 NIV

■ "You're blessed when you're at the end of your rope. With less of you there is more of God and his rule.

"You're blessed when you feel you've lost what is most dear to you. Only then can you be embraced by the One most dear to you.

"You're blessed when you're content with just who you are—no more, no less. That's the moment you find yourselves proud owners of everything that can't be bought.

"You're blessed when you've worked up a good appetite for God. He's food and drink in the best meal you'll ever eat.

"You're blessed when you care. At the moment of being 'care-full,' you find your-selves cared for.

"You're blessed when you get your inside world—your mind and heart—put right. Then you can see God in the outside world.

"You're blessed when you can show people how to cooperate instead of compete or fight. That's when you discover who you really are, and your place in God's family.

"You're blessed when your commitment to God provokes persecution. The persecution drives you even deeper into God's kingdom."

MATTHEW 5:3–10 MSG

TRUSTING GOD'S PLAN

"I am with you and will watch over you
wherever you go, and I will bring you back to
this land. I will not leave you until I have done
what I have promised you."

GENESIS 28:15 NIV

Those who know your name will trust in you,
for you, LORD, have never forsaken those
who seek you.

PSALM 9:10 NIV

You, LORD, are the light that keeps me safe.
I am not afraid of anyone.
    You protect me, and I have no fears.

PSALM 27:1 CEV

■ Yet I am poor and needy;
     may the Lord think of me.
You are my help and my deliverer;
     O my God, do not delay.

PSALM 40:17 NIV

■ Where can I go from your Spirit?
     Where can I flee from your presence?
If I go up to the heavens, you are there;
     if I make my bed in the depths,
     you are there.
If I rise on the wings of the dawn,
     if I settle on the far side of the sea,
even there your hand will guide me,
     your right hand will hold me fast.

PSALM 139:7–10 NIV

The LORD directs the steps of the godly.
He delights in every detail of their lives.

PSALM 37:23 NLT

One thing I ask of the LORD,
    this is what I seek:
that I may dwell in the house of the LORD
    all the days of my life,
to gaze upon the beauty of the LORD
    and to seek him in his temple.
For in the day of trouble
    he will keep me safe in his dwelling;
he will hide me in the shelter of his
    tabernacle and set me high upon a rock.

PSALM 27:4 – 5 NIV

BELIEVING IN A FUTURE HOPE

■ Now we know that if the earthly tent we live in is destroyed, we have a building from God, an eternal house in heaven, not built by human hands.

2 CORINTHIANS 5:1 NIV

■ "In my Father's house are many rooms; if it were not so, I would have told you. I am going there to prepare a place for you."

JOHN 14:2 NIV

■ Our citizenship is in heaven. And we eagerly await a Savior from there, the Lord Jesus Christ.

PHILIPPIANS 3:20 NIV

For this we declare to you by a word from the Lord, that we who are alive, who are left until the coming of the Lord, will not precede those who have fallen asleep. For the Lord himself will descend from heaven with a cry of command, with the voice of an archangel, and with the sound of the trumpet of God. And the dead in Christ will rise first. Then we who are alive, who are left, will be caught up together with them in the clouds to meet the Lord in the air, and so we will always be with the Lord. Therefore encourage one another with these words.

1 THESSALONIANS 4:15–18 ESV

"He will wipe every tear from their eyes. There will be no more death or mourning or crying or pain, for the old order of things has passed away."

REVELATION 21:4 NIV

■ Then I heard what seemed to be the
voice of a great multitude, like the roar of
many waters and like the sound of mighty
peals of thunder, crying out, "Hallelujah!
For the Lord our God the Almighty reigns."

REVELATION 19:6 ESV

■ "For the Lamb at the center of the throne
will be their shepherd; he will lead them to
springs of living water. And God will wipe
away every tear from their eyes."

REVELATION 7:17 NIV

■ The LORD All-Powerful will destroy the power
of death and wipe away all tears. No longer
will his people be insulted everywhere.
　　　The LORD has spoken!

ISAIAH 25:8 CEV

REFRESHING YOUR HEART

The Holy Spirit helps us in our weakness.
For example, we don't know what God
wants us to pray for. But the Holy Spirit
prays for us with groanings that cannot be
expressed in words.

ROMANS 8:26 NLT

The LORD is near to all who call on him,
to all who call on him in truth.
He fulfills the desires of those who fear him;
he hears their cry and saves them.

PSALM 145:18–19 NIV

On the day I called, you answered me,
you increased my strength of soul.

PSALM 138:3 NRSV

■ Let me abide in your tent forever,
find refuge under the shelter of your wings.

PSALM 61:4 NRSV

■ Search me, O God, and know my heart;
test me and know my anxious thoughts.

PSALM 139:23 NLT

■ Let all bitterness and wrath and anger and
clamor and slander be put away from you,
along with all malice.

EPHESIANS 4:31 ESV

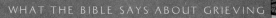 I am still confident of this:

> I will see the goodness of the LORD
>
> in the land of the living.

Wait for the LORD;

> be strong and take heart
>
> and wait for the LORD.

PSALM 27:13–14 NIV

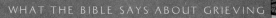 In peace I will lie down and sleep,

for you alone, O LORD, will keep me safe.

PSALM 4:8 NLT

ONE MOMENT
AT A TIME

CLINGING
TO FAITH

1. Consider this: C. S. Lewis wrote in
A Grief Observed: "Can a mortal ask
questions which God finds unanswerable?
Quite easily, I should think. All nonsense
questions are unanswerable. How many
hours are there in a mile? Is yellow square or
round? Probably half the questions we ask—
half of our great theological and metaphysical
problems—are like that. . . . When I lay these
questions before God I get no answer, but a
rather special sort of 'no answer.' It is not the
locked door. It is more like a silent, certainly
not uncompassionate gaze. As though He
shook his head not in refusal but waiving

the question. Like, 'Peace, child; you don't understand.' "

2. Look for growth. God can use pain to help you grow. Many Bible characters grew closest to God through their darkest hours.

3. Hold on to what you know. When you are in pain, your emotions are screaming—sometimes drowning out the truths of God that you discovered when life wasn't so hard. Hold on to the truths of God's character—those haven't changed even though your circumstances have. Though you may have trouble seeing it, God is still good, still wise, still loving, and still with you.

CHAPTER 10

KNOWING GOD DURING THIS TIME

There were times in the months following my mom's death that I was angry at God. I worked through it, though, and realize now that God is truly my best Friend. While I have family and friends, they will all fail me—and eventually die. And one day I will, too. The thought used to scare me, but the closer I grow to God, the less it does. God is my ultimate source of comfort and strength, and without Him I would truly have no hope.

■ Capri, age 19, Nevada ■

KNOWING GOD'S LOVE

■ I am convinced that neither death nor life, neither angels nor demons, neither the present nor the future, nor any powers, neither height nor depth, nor anything else in all creation, will be able to separate us from the love of God that is in Christ Jesus our Lord.

ROMANS 8:38–39 NIV

■ The LORD is good, a refuge in times of trouble. He cares for those who trust in him.

NAHUM 1:7 NIV

■ We know what real love is because Jesus gave up his life for us.

1 JOHN 3:16 NLT

■ God put his love on the line for us by offering his Son in sacrificial death while we were of no use whatever to him.

ROMANS 5:8 MSG

■ Great is his faithfulness;
     his mercies begin afresh each morning.
I say to myself, "The LORD is my inheritance;
     therefore, I will hope in him!"

LAMENTATIONS 3:23–24 NLT

■ In a desert land he found him,
     in a barren and howling waste.
He shielded him and cared for him;
     he guarded him as the apple of his eye.

DEUTERONOMY 32:10 NIV

■ Know therefore that the LORD your God is God; he is the faithful God, keeping his covenant of love to a thousand generations of those who love him and keep his commands.

DEUTERONOMY 7:9 NIV

■ "For God so loved the world, that he gave his only Son, that whoever believes in him should not perish but have eternal life."

JOHN 3:16 ESV

■ I pray that you, being rooted and established in love, may have power, together with all the saints, to grasp how wide and long and high and deep is the love of Christ, and to know this love that surpasses knowledge—that you may be filled to the measure of all the fullness of God.

EPHESIANS 3:17–19 NIV

GRIPPING GOD'S GRACE

You surely don't think much of God's wonderful goodness or of his patience and willingness to put up with you. Don't you know that the reason God is good to you is because he wants you to turn to him?

ROMANS 2:4 CEV

"But in your great mercy you did not put an end to them or abandon them, for you are a gracious and merciful God."

NEHEMIAH 9:31 NIV

"You have granted me life and steadfast love, and your care has preserved my spirit."

JOB 10:12 ESV

■ I always thank God for you because of his grace given you in Christ Jesus. For in him you have been enriched in every way—in all your speaking and in all your knowledge—because our testimony about Christ was confirmed in you. Therefore you do not lack any spiritual gift as you eagerly wait for our Lord Jesus Christ to be revealed. He will keep you strong to the end, so that you will be blameless on the day of our Lord Jesus Christ.

1 CORINTHIANS 1:4–8 NIV

■ For you are a people holy to the LORD your God. The LORD your God has chosen you out of all the peoples on the face of the earth to be his people, his treasured possession.

DEUTERONOMY 7:6 NIV

■ For it is by grace you have been saved, through faith—and this not from yourselves, it is the gift of God—not by works, so that no one can boast.

 EPHESIANS 2:8–9 NIV

■ "Repent, then, and turn to God, so that your sins may be wiped out, that times of refreshing may come from the Lord."

ACTS 3:19 NIV

■ God is able to make all grace abound to you, so that in all things at all times, having all that you need, you will abound in every good work.

2 CORINTHIANS 9:8 NIV

■ Whenever we are in need, we should come bravely before the throne of our merciful God. There we will be treated with undeserved kindness, and we will find help.

HEBREWS 4:16 CEV

EXPERIENCING GOD'S CONCERN

How precious are your thoughts about me,
   O God.
They cannot be numbered!
I can't even count them;
   they outnumber the grains of sand!
And when I wake up,
   you are still with me!

PSALM 139:17–18 NLT

"Before I shaped you in the womb,
   I knew all about you.
Before you saw the light of day,
   I had holy plans for you:
A prophet to the nations—
   that's what I had in mind for you."

JEREMIAH 1:5 MSG

■ He gave his life to free us from every kind of sin, to cleanse us, and to make us his very own people, totally committed to doing good deeds.

TITUS 2:14 NLT

■ Praise the God and Father of our Lord Jesus Christ for the spiritual blessings that Christ has brought us from heaven! Before the world was created, God had Christ choose us to live with him and to be his holy and innocent and loving people. God was kind and decided that Christ would choose us to be God's own adopted children. God was very kind to us because of the Son he dearly loves, and so we should praise God.

EPHESIANS 1:3–6 CEV

"I no longer call you servants, because a servant does not know his master's business. Instead, I have called you friends, for everything that I learned from my Father I have made known to you."

JOHN 15:15 NIV

For you are all children of God through faith in Christ Jesus.

GALATIANS 3:26 NLT

But to all who did receive him, who believed in his name, he gave the right to become children of God.

JOHN 1:12 ESV

■ For all who are led by the Spirit of God are
children of God.

So you have not received a spirit that
makes you fearful slaves. Instead, you received
God's Spirit when he adopted you as his own
children. Now we call him, "Abba, Father."

ROMANS 8:14–15 NLT

■ You keep track of all my sorrows.
You have collected all my tears in your bottle.
You have recorded each one in your book.

PSALM 56:8 NLT

HOLDING ON TO GOD'S STRENGTH

Do you not know?
Have you not heard?
The LORD is the everlasting God,
>   the Creator of the ends of the earth.
He will not grow tired or weary,
>   and his understanding no one
>   can fathom.
He gives strength to the weary
>   and increases the power of the weak.
Even youths grow tired and weary,
>   and young men stumble and fall;
>   but those who hope in the LORD will
>   renew their strength.
They will soar on wings like eagles;
>   they will run and not grow weary,
>   they will walk and not be faint.

ISAIAH 40:28–31 NIV

■ You are my hiding place; you will protect me from trouble and surround me with songs of deliverance.

PSALM 32:7 NIV

■ Then Jesus said, "Come to me, all of you who are weary and carry heavy burdens, and I will give you rest. Take my yoke upon you. Let me teach you, because I am humble and gentle at heart, and you will find rest for your souls. For my yoke is easy to bear, and the burden I give you is light."

MATTHEW 11:28–30 NLT

■ But the Lord stood by me and gave me strength.

2 TIMOTHY 4:17 NRSV

■ For he will command his angels concerning you to guard you in all your ways.

PSALM 91:11 NIV

■ I look up to the mountains;
    does my strength come from mountains?
No, my strength comes from GOD,
    who made heaven, and earth,
    and mountains.

PSALM 121:1–2 MSG

■ Be gracious to me, O LORD, for I am languishing; heal me, O LORD, for my bones are troubled.

My soul also is greatly troubled.
But you, O LORD—how long?
Turn, O LORD, deliver my life;
save me for the sake of your steadfast love.

PSALM 6:2–4 ESV

STRENGTHENING YOUR FAITH

◼ I rise before dawn and cry for help;
I hope in your words.

PSALM 119:147 ESV

◼ My comfort in my suffering is this:
Your promise preserves my life.

PSALM 119:50 NIV

◼ I acknowledged my sin to you,
and I did not cover my iniquity;
I said, "I will confess my transgressions
to the LORD," and you forgave the iniquity
of my sin.

PSALM 32:5 ESV

■ Your word is a lamp to my feet and a light to my path.

PSALM 119:105 ESV

■ This is a trustworthy saying that deserves full acceptance (and for this we labor and strive), that we have put our hope in the living God, who is the Savior of all men, and especially of those who believe.

1 TIMOTHY 4:9–10 NIV

■ Do your best to improve your faith. You can do this by adding goodness, understanding, self-control, patience, devotion to God, concern for others, and love. If you keep growing in this way, it will show that what you know about our Lord Jesus Christ has made your lives useful and meaningful.

2 PETER 1:5–8 CEV

ONE MOMENT
AT A TIME

DEEPENING
YOUR FAITH

1. Read a book. Christian bookstores offer many titles that can help you grow in intimacy with God through your time of grief.

2. Become better acquainted with Job. Few people experience the extreme loss and pain the biblical character Job faced. While Job's friends and family were unable to comfort him, his faith in God was ultimately strengthened. Toward the end of the account, he says to God: "My ears had heard of you but now my eyes have seen you" (Job 42:5 NIV). Read Job and identify with what he learned.

3. Consider creating a blog or journal. Your emotional highs and lows can yield tremendous growth. Regular writing can help you organize your thoughts and process through the lessons God may be teaching you.

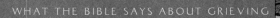

CHAPTER 11

LINGERING HURTS

Sometimes my pain haunts me. I'll be doing well for a number of days, and then a song, a news story, or even a smell will set me off. Without warning I'm lost to the renewed pain and tears that suddenly engulf me. I'm probably most surprised that the heartache is just as strong today as it was months ago. It seems like I should be getting over this by now. Is this normal?

■ Karla, age 31, Iowa ■

COPING WITH ENDURING PAIN

■ I'll never forget the trouble, the utter lostness,
the taste of ashes, the poison I've
swallowed.
I remember it all—oh, how well I
remember—the feeling of hitting
the bottom.
But there's one other thing I remember,
and remembering, I keep a grip on hope:
GOD's loyal love couldn't have run out,
his merciful love couldn't have dried up.

LAMENTATIONS 3:19–22 MSG

■ Bring joy to your servant, for to you, O Lord,
I lift up my soul.

PSALM 86:4 NIV

■ I learned God-worship when my pride
was shattered.

Heart-shattered lives ready for love
don't for a moment escape God's notice.

PSALM 51:17 MSG

■ For he has not ignored or belittled the
suffering of the needy.

He has not turned his back on them,
but has listened to their cries for help.

PSALM 22:24 NLT

■ Pray that our LORD will make us strong
and give us peace.

PSALM 29:11 CEV

Praise be to the God and Father of our Lord Jesus Christ, the Father of compassion and the God of all comfort.

2 CORINTHIANS 1:3 NIV

REMINDING YOURSELF OF GOD'S CONSTANT CARE

■ So let's *do* it—full of belief, confident that we're presentable inside and out. Let's keep a firm grip on the promises that keep us going. He always keeps his word.

HEBREWS 10:22–23 MSG

■ The LORD your God will always be at your side, and he will never abandon you.

DEUTERONOMY 31:6 CEV

■ The LORD is my rock, my fortress and my deliverer; my God is my rock, in whom I take refuge.

He is my shield and the horn of my salvation, my stronghold.

PSALM 18:2 NIV

■ "The eternal God is your refuge,
      and underneath are the everlasting arms.
He will drive out your enemy before you,
      saying, 'Destroy him!' "

DEUTERONOMY 33:27 NIV

■ "Though the mountains be shaken and the
hills be removed, yet my unfailing love for you
will not be shaken nor my covenant of
peace be removed," says the LORD, who
has compassion on you.

ISAIAH 54:10 NIV

■ Give thanks to the LORD, for he is good!
      His faithful love endures forever.

PSALM 107:1 NLT

EXPERIENCING NEW HOPE

■ For you have been my hope, O Sovereign LORD, my confidence since my youth.

PSALM 71:5 NIV

■ Being confident of this, that he who began a good work in you will carry it on to completion until the day of Christ Jesus.

PHILIPPIANS 1:6 NIV

■ But you, O Sovereign LORD, deal well with me for your name's sake; out of the goodness of your love, deliver me.

For I am poor and needy, and my heart is wounded within me.

PSALM 109:21–22 NIV

■ To all who mourn in Israel, he will give a crown of beauty for ashes, a joyous blessing instead of mourning, festive praise instead of despair. In their righteousness, they will be like great oaks that the LORD has planted for his own glory.

ISAIAH 61:3 NLT

■ Why am I discouraged? Why am I restless? I trust you! And I will praise you again because you help me.

PSALM 42:5 CEV

■ And this same God who takes care of me will supply all your needs from his glorious riches, which have been given to us in Christ Jesus.

PHILIPPIANS 4:19 NLT

■ Trust in the LORD and do good.
   Then you will live safely in the land
and prosper.

PSALM 37:3 NLT

■ Praise the LORD!
Oh give thanks to the LORD, for he is good,
   for his steadfast love endures forever!

PSALM 106:1 ESV

■ Consider it pure joy, my brothers, whenever
you face trials of many kinds, because you
know that the testing of your faith develops
perseverance. Perseverance must finish
its work so that you may be mature and
complete, not lacking anything.

JAMES 1:2–4 NIV

ONE MOMENT
AT A TIME

SCARS HEAL
SLOWLY

1. Be patient with others. Friends and family may not understand why you are still grieving. Sometimes they may be insensitive, and other times they may be afraid to bring up your loss for fear of upsetting you. Either way, remember that they love you and probably mean well.

2. Believe life is still worth living. Work through the difficult feelings, but don't dwell on them without purpose. Embrace the life God has given you.

3. Celebrate with a memorial a year after your loss. Grief does not follow a calendar or have an ending date. Planning a private or public memorial after some time has passed can help you celebrate this person's life a little further removed from the sting of the initial loss.

4. Monitor your media. Music lyrics, movies, and TV shows can conjure up difficult emotions. Choose your entertainment carefully.

Look for all the
What the Bible Says About…
books from Barbour Publishing

What the Bible Says about
DIVORCE
ISBN 978-1-59789-995-6

What the Bible Says about
MARRIAGE
ISBN 978-1-59789-993-2

What the Bible Says about
MONEY
ISBN 978-1-59789-992-5

192 pages / 3 ¾" × 6" / $4.97 each

Available wherever Christian books are sold.